REVELATION

From the Bible-Teaching Ministry of
STEPHEN DAVEY

UNDERSTANDING REVELATION

Author: Stephen Davey

Cover Design & Body Layout: Kristin Preston

Photo of Stephen: Tierney Riggs Braddock, Raleigh-Durham, NC
(https://www.tierneyriggsphotography.com/)

ISBN 978-1-944189-32-7

© 2019 Stephen Davey. All rights reserved.
Unless otherwise noted, all Scripture quotations are from the New American Standard Bible®, Copyright © 1960, 1962, 1963, 1968, 1971, 1972, 1973, 1975, 1995 by the Lockman Foundation.
Used by permission.

Consideration has been made to footnote sources whenever necessary. In the case of any unintentional omission, future editions will include appropriate notations.

UNDERSTANDING REVELATION

The Old Lie

Rhonda Byrne is the author of the once popular book entitled The Secret. It uncovers what she claims to have stumbled onto at the end of 2004.

At that time, everything in Rhonda's life had fallen apart—physically, emotionally, and financially. She was in "total despair." Her father had died suddenly and she was worried about her grief-stricken mother. She said, "I wept and wept and wept." This was when Rhonda's daughter gave her a copy of *The Science of Getting Rich*, a book written in 1910 by Wallace D. Wattles.

"Something inside of me had me turn the pages one by one, and I can still remember my tears hitting the pages as I was reading it," Rhonda says. "It gave me a glimpse of The Secret. It was like a flame inside of my heart. And with every day since, it's just become a raging fire of wanting to share all of this with the world."

Rhonda claims to have spent hours tracing the concept of The Secret through history—all the way from 3500 B.C. to the present day. She says, "Since I discovered The Secret, every single moment of my entire life has changed, and I am living my life for the first time."

So, what is The Secret? The Secret is the law of attraction, which is the principle that "like attracts like." Rhonda calls it "the most powerful law in the universe that never stops working." She goes on to explain, "What we do is attract into our lives the things we want, and that's based on what we're thinking and feeling . . . this principle explains that we create our own circumstances through our own thoughts. Our thoughts are the most powerful things we have here on earth."

The truth about The Secret is that you do not choose to follow God; you choose to recognize that you are God. You are divine; you are sovereign. Satan made a similar claim to Eve:

"Eve, I have a secret . . . eat this fruit and you shall be as God."

It doesn't really surprise me that this kind of thinking has the world deceived. What surprises me is that this is the same corrupt, self-deceived concept within the prosperity movement of the church whose false teachers have repackaged this age-old lie into supposed revelation from God.

These false teachers are leading people into a misguided, self-centered belief system that corresponds to the lie of the enemy that people are really gods and whatever they say has the power to create reality. This is the secret people need to learn - they are really a god and they can create, with their words and thoughts, whatever they want.

Let me quote a couple of leading spokesmen. Creflo Dollar recently said,

Everything produces after its own kind. Horses get horses and dogs get dogs and Gods produced gods! . . . Ya'll didn't hear that. Horses produce horses and dogs produce dogs and Gods produced gods! . . . And then God produced more gods with flesh and then gods with

flesh produced more gods with flesh. And then gods with flesh produced more gods with flesh until THE God of gods with flesh showed up one day with flesh and dwelt among the other gods with flesh to demonstrate to the other gods how to have authority over the flesh! . . . This is the history the religious church wants to hide away from you so you don't know who you really are![1]

In other words, this is the secret the church has kept away from you. You are a little god in the flesh, created by THE God, and you have the same power He has to create your own destiny and reality.

Another false teacher, by the name of Kenneth Copeland, has taught for years this same concept. He said some time ago:

You can have whatever you say! In fact, what you are saying is exactly what you are getting now. If you are living in poverty, change what you are saying. It will change what you have . . . discipline everything you do, everything you say . . . God will be obligated to meet your needs.[2]

In other words, speak it into existence. You have the power of God to create your own reality.

I was frankly amazed as literally millions of people purchased *The Prayer of Jabez*. I don't think the author of this little book is a false teacher. But whether this author intended it or not, people were swept up in the natural instinct to find some secret. This became some special set of words that were guaranteed to work. The subtle implication was that praying this prayer; speaking these same words would bring to us what we want.

My friends, there is no incantation; no special prayer that guarantees you anything. There is no secret that will heal your diseases, bring global peace, put money in your bank account, and a new car in your garage.

What seems tragic to me is that the church often softens the soil in people's hearts to receive false doctrine. There's a new gospel that is becoming mainstream but it's filled with errors. All of these false teachers hold out the same lie—ultimately, you are divine You can act like God because you are God. You can control your body and your bank account with your own wishes. You can speak your destiny.

"Eat this Eve . . . and you shall be as wise as God."

I want to state as plainly as I can: this is not some new secret or new revelation. Teaching like this an old lie! You are not God. You and I are sinners in need of our Single Savior!

The Old Revelation

It's time for the church to learn - not new revelation, but the old revelation. I don't want to discover the power of my words. I want to know the power of His words. You do not need a revelation from Stephen Davey. You and I need a revelation of and through and by and about Jesus Christ— who was and is and always shall be the singular Savior.

We need to return to the old revelation of God's Word.

In your New testament, that's exactly what the book of Revelation is. In Revelation chapter 1, the very first five words say,

The Revelation of Jesus Christ . . .

Don't ever forget that opening statement as you seek to understand the book of Revelation. You'll encounter signs and bowls and trumpets and resurrections and judgments and wars and visions. But at its core, the book of Revelation is revelation about Jesus. It's a revelation of Jesus Christ. It has as its grandest theme the person Jesus Christ. It uncovers as its greatest treasure the supremacy of Jesus Christ. It builds upon its most profound thesis—the sovereignty of Jesus Christ.

Above everything, this is the revelation of Jesus Christ. This is revelation that comes from Jesus Christ. He is the One doing the revealing. But it's also the the revelation of Jesus Christ in that Christ is the One being revealed. Both are true. Jesus Christ is both the source of revelation and the grand subject revealed.[3] This revelation is from and about our sovereign Lord.

Despite the fact that Revelation is by and about Jesus Christ, it can be difficult to understand, and it seems at times to be unapproachable. To help frame your thinking about the book of Revelation, I've outlined some questions about the book to assist you in your study.

Seven Basic Questions About Revelation

First: What is true revelation?

The answer to this first question is found in the meaning of the word. "Revelation" is the transliteration of the Greek word, "apokalupsis," which means, "to unveil; to uncover that which was previously hidden".[4]

Is it not ironic that the book of the Bible that means "revealed and open" is considered by many Christians to be the most mysterious and closed book of all? However, this book is not called, "The Mystery of Jesus Christ" or "The Puzzle of Jesus Christ," but literally, "The Unveiling of Jesus Christ" or "The Open Book of Jesus Christ".[5] Yet many fear to open it and read.

Without a doubt, the greatest obstacle in understanding the book of Revelation is the approach one takes. There are four primary approaches to this revelation.

First, there is the **preterist approach** to understanding Revelation. This approach says that Revelation is simply a history book. This view believes that, with few exceptions, the events in the book of Revelation have already taken place. As a result, those who hold this view have to spiritualize the fall of the Temple in A.D. 70 as the time when Christ returned. The trouble with this is that Christ did not even appear. In addition, they leave no room to interpret a literal fulfillment of the seals and trumpets and bowl judgments. It is interesting that this approach seems to overlook the clear declaration of the first verses and the last verses of Revelation, which clearly state that this is a book of prophecy, not history.

The second approach to interpreting Revelation is the **historicist approach**. Those who follow this approach believe that all the prophecies have been fulfilled sometime during the past 2,000 years. This approach is interesting since they have to find historical connections to things and events, which requires a very good imagination. They see the locusts referring to monks and friars. They see Muhammad as the fallen star and Alaric the Goth as the first trumpet; Elizabeth I as the first bowl, Martin Luther as the angel of Sardis, Adolf Hitler as the red horse, etc., etc.[6]

The third approach is the **idealist approach**. This view basically says that Revelation is a set of ideal principles related to the struggle between good and evil. It allegorizes the entire book as a spiritual conflict and says that none of it relates to literal events in history or in the future. The tribulation is simply one's internal conflict with sin and pain; the return of Christ takes place in one's own heart and mind.[7]

The fourth approach, and the one I follow, is one that takes the book of Revelation at face value—it is called the **futurist approach**. This view understands Revelation as a prophetic account of actual future events, specifically focused on the end of this age. One author commented that this is simply the natural result of a straightforward reading of the book, while the other three approaches are often forced to resort to allegorizing or spiritualizing the text to sustain their interpretations.[8]

We interpret the prophets literally. We take them at face value. It should be no surprise then, to do the same with the book of Revelation. Half of the book of Revelation is actually references to the Old Testament. What has been concealed is now revealed! 278 of the 404 verses in Revelation are a reference to something already referenced in the Old Testament.

Willmington's survey of Revelation cataloged them all. I would not want his job, but I am glad he did it. In his work he catalogued the Old Testament references in the book of Revelation as including:

- 13 from Genesis;
- 27 from Exodus;
- 4 from Leviticus;
- 3 from Numbers;
- 10 from Deuteronomy;
- 1 apiece from Joshua, Judges, and II Samuel;
- 6 from I Kings;
- 1 from both I Chronicles and Nehemiah;
- 43 from Psalms;
- 2 from Proverbs;
- 79 from Isaiah;
- 22 from Jeremiah;
- 43 from Ezekiel;
- 53 from Daniel;
- 2 from Hosea;

- 8 from Joel;
- 9 from Amos;
- 1 from Habakkuk;
- 2 from Zephaniah;
- 15 from Zechariah;
- 1 from Malachi.[9]

Half the problem for the interpreter is solved if he will interpret the Old Testament literally—taking it at face value.

So what is the book of Revelation? It is the last word of prophecy. It is the capstone of prophetic revelation.

Second: What is this revelation about?

John writes in the first few words, that this is the the Revelation of Jesus Christ. It is the revelation by Him, but most importantly, of Him. If you study Revelation, you'll discover in this book who He is and what He says and what He does.

This is the old revelation to which we must return.

- He is Jesus Christ (Revelation 1:1).
- He is the ruler of the kings of the earth (Revelation 1:5).
- He is the First and the Last (Revelation 2:8).
- He is the Son of God (Revelation 2:18).
- He is the One who searches the minds and hearts (Revelation 2:23).
- He is the One who has the key of David (Revelation 3:7).

- He is the One who opens the door that no one can shut (Revelation 3:7).
- He is the Amen (Revelation 3:14).
- He is the faithful and true Witness (Revelation 3:14).
- He is the Lion of the tribe of Judah (Revelation 5:5).
- He is the Root of David (Revelation 5:5).
- He is the true One (Revelation 6:10).
- He is the holy One (Revelation 6:10).
- He is the Lord (Revelation 11:8).
- He is the Christ (Revelation 11:15).
- He is the Lamb (Revelation 12:11).
- He is the King (Revelation 15:3).
- He is the Word of God (Revelation 19:13).
- He is the King of Kings and Lord of Lords (Revelation 19:16).
- He is the Alpha and the Omega (Revelation 21:6).
- He is the beginning and the end (Revelation 22:13).
- He is the bright and morning star (Revelation 22:16).
- He is the Lord Jesus (Revelation 22:20).

Each title given to Jesus Christ in Revelation is a revelation of redemptive truth.

Christ is called the Alpha and the Omega, which are the

first and last letters of the Greek alphabet. These carry with them the suggestion of literature—signifying perhaps, that in the literature of revelation, the Bible, of which Christ is the substance, that He is the truth from the very first letter of the Bible to the very last letter.

He is also called the First and the Last—a title which seems to carry the idea of history, and thus would mean that Christ was the crown of all of history.

He is also called the beginning and the end, which appears to have reference to creation and time, so that He is at both ends of time, as it were, and is the cause and maintainer of creation.

He is called the first begotten in chapter 1—a reference to His resurrection.

He is called the Lamb in chapter 5, as well as 26 other times in the book—a title which speaks of redemption. He is the Single Savior.

He is called the Lion of the tribe of Judah, which refers to His royalty.

He is called the root and offspring of David—meaning He was before David and after David.

He is the morning star in chapter 22, which tells us He will usher in the eternal day.

This entire book gathers around to exalt Him.[10] This is the old revelation. This is the truth from God. The Carpenter of Nazareth is the King of the world. The crucified Jew is both Lamb and Lord of the universe![11]

Third: Who is the audience for this revelation?

John goes on to write in verse Revelation 1:11 that this revelation from God is to be shown to,

> *. . . His bond-servants . . .*

To further exalt and glorify His Son, the Father granted to a special group of people the privilege of understanding this book. John describes these people with this word translated "bond-servants," from the Greek word that literally means "slave".[12] I agree with one author that the word "slave" should not be watered down or weakened to suit our tastes. It was common in John's day for a person to sell himself into slavery in a pagan temple to serve the idol.[13]

In Old Testament days, during the celebration of Jubilee when all the indentured servants in Israel were liberated and their debts were cleared, if a slave so loved his master that he wanted to remain in his service for the rest of his life, he would be taken to the door of the Tabernacle. There, his ear would be pierced and ringed, thus signifying that he was a servant who had chosen his master out of love and loyalty.

This was in the mind of Paul when he referred to himself as the slave of Jesus Christ. The revelation of Christ is revealed to His loyal and loving slaves. Those who refuse to acknowledge the mastery of Christ cannot,

> *. . . accept the things of the Spirit of God, for they are foolishness to him; and he cannot understand them, because they are spiritually appraised. (I Corinthians 2:14)*

The unbelieving skeptic will consider Revelation a compilation of nonsense. But the believer, who is willingly enslaved out of love and loyalty to Christ, will understand and believe the prophetic truths about the future of the world.

Fourth: How is the revelation communicated?

Notice the last part of Revelation 1:1:

> *. . . and He sent and communicated it by His angel to His bond-servant John,*

You might think, "Isn't that dangerous? Isn't that risky? Haven't we been warned of gospels delivered by angels? Spirit beings delivered the religions of Islam and Mormonism."

There are angels everywhere in this book. They are referred to 71 times! Someone made the comment that 1 out of every 4 references to angels are in the book of Revelation.

This brings us to a fifth question that needs to be asked and answered.

Fifth: How is this revelation authenticated?

Revelation 1:2 tells us it is authenticated by,

"the word of God and to the testimony of Jesus Christ, even to all that [John] saw."

Notice the three-fold testimony.

First, it is authenticated by ***the word of God***. In other words, this revelation is consistent with the rest of scripture.

So, compare scripture with scripture; let scripture define and explain scripture.

Furthermore, there is ***the testimony of Jesus Christ***. The apostle Paul did not warn people of hearing truth from angels. In fact, he did not say that an angel could not deliver the gospel. He did say, in Galatians 1:8, ". . . even if . . . an angel from heaven, should preach to you a [different] gospel . . . he is to be accursed!" What does the angel say about Christ? Many religions say that Christ is someone other than God alone. They are saying, "You are god . . . you are the spirit of Jesus." We authenticate the testimony of John by the testimony of scripture and of Christ.

The third verification in the text is the eyewitness of John himself—***even to all that [John] saw***. If this revelation were being tried in court as true or not, the defense attorney would present the written testimony of God the Father, refer to spoken testimony of God the Son, and show how they correspond perfectly with one another, and then call to the stand an eyewitness. We will then hear John the apostle say, "This is what I saw!"

Look at Revelation 1:12-13.

> *Then I turned to see the voice that was speaking with me. And having turned I saw seven golden lampstands; and in the middle of the lampstands I saw one like a son of man, clothed in a robe reaching to the feet . . .*

Skip to verse 17a.

When I saw Him, I fell at His feet like a dead man. . . .

Turn to chapter 5, verse 1.

I saw in the right hand of Him who sat on the throne a book written inside and on the back . . .

Notice chapter 21, verse 1.

Then I saw a new heaven and a new earth . . .

Forty-four times, John will say effectively, "I saw! I can verify the testimony of this revelation with my own eyes."[14]

There are people who have flat-lined on a hospital bed or at an accident scene and were revived after some time, only to tell incredible accounts of what they saw in heaven and for some, even in hell. Their books fly off the shelves in sales. Why? Their testimony is not, "This is what I read," or "This is what I heard." Their testimony, right or wrong, is all the more compelling because they are saying, "This is what I saw."

This is the most descriptive, tell-all eyewitness account of heaven anywhere, with an eyewitness who, with passion and urgency, says, "You need to know what I saw."

Let me answer another question.

Sixth: Why should I study this revelation?

John continues in Revelation 1:3, saying,

Blessed is he who reads and those who hear the words of the prophecy, and heed the things which are written in it; . . .

This is the only book in the Bible that promises special blessing for those who do three things.

Blessed are those who read it. This was probably an encouragement to the lector—the one responsible to read publicly in the synagogue or church the writings of scripture.[15] In the early days of the church, the limited number of copies of scripture demanded that they be read publicly. This is unlike today, when completed scriptures are so commonplace.

I have on one of my bookshelves in my study at home, a framed sheet of notebook paper with handwritten Chinese characters written across it in neat lines. It was given to me by missionaries from China. This sheet of paper is a page out of someone's handwritten Bible. It is so special to me. For one thing, it convicts me as I sit surrounded by Bibles and commentaries. I have 80 commentaries on this one book of Revelation—each containing the text of scripture. I read from 60 of them in preparation for teaching through Revelation. That Chinese believer probably does not have one complete copy of scripture, and what he has was written down as fast as he could while he borrowed a copy from someone else.

The apostle John knew that this revelation was critical. And he added the incentive of God's blessing upon all who would read it aloud to others.

The blessing extended not only to the reader, but to the hearer. And not just to the hearer, but to the doer. Notice that those who also heed the words, obey them. This echoes the writings of James, who declared as blessed the believer who not only heard the word, but did what it commanded (James 1:25).

Let me add one more question.

Seventh: Why does this revelation matter?

The last part of verse 3, adds this urgent point,

. . . for the time is near.

The word translated "time," in this verse, does not refer to a clock or a calendar. This word is "*kairos,*" which refers to epochs or seasons. John is saying, "The epoch is near. It's at hand. The next great era of God's redemptive history is close at hand. The return of Christ is imminent."

The urgency of Revelation points to the return of Christ. The risen Savior who appeared to John is the Sovereign who will return with His triumphant church at the end of the book. Everything points to His literal return.

The era of the single Savior is not over—it is just about to begin with greater majesty and might than we could ever imagine.

Jesus Christ says in Revelation:

- "I am coming quickly." (3:11)
- "And behold, I am coming quickly. Blessed is he who heeds the words of the prophecy of this book." (22:7)

- "Behold, I am coming quickly, and My reward is with Me." (22:12)
- "Yes, I am coming quickly." (22:20)

And John shouts, as the book ends,

Amen. Come! (Revelation 20:20)

"Come on then—we're waiting and we're watching this time!"

Don't ever forget that there were over 100 prophecies about the first coming of Christ and everybody missed it! The people missed it! There are over 200 prophecies about what is going to happen next—and you do not want to miss it. Do not miss Him because of unbelief.

Conclusion

How do you find Jesus? There is this old revelation which reveals Him. This is the answer; the guidebook; the mystery revealed. This is the revelation that exalts and magnifies a single Savior—and you are not it! Neither am I. It is Jesus Christ, who is coming again.

Mrs. Phoebe Knapp was a personal friend of Fanny Crosby, the famous hymn writer. Phoebe was a hymn writer herself, but often provided the melodies that Crosby used with her hymn texts. One of the most famous of Phoebe Knapp's hymn melodies was the one composed for Fannie Crosby's hymn text, "Blessed Assurance, Jesus is Mine."

Even more interesting to me is the fact that Phoebe Knapp was the wife of Joseph Knapp, the founder and president of the Metropolitan Life Insurance Company. Phoebe would later say, "It's a wonderful thing to have insurance for life, but a far better thing to have assurance for life hereafter."

This blessed assurance is only found when you ignore the claims of those who tell you they've found some new secret or some new revelation. Return to the old revelation that exalts and magnifies our wonderful Savior.

Endnotes

[1] Creflo Dollar, "The Creative Ability of Words," http://www.forgottenword.org/dollar.html, Tape from his ministry, Product Number: 8432091.

[2] Ken Copeland, "The Laws of Prosperity," pp. 98, 101, quoted by D. R. McConnell in A Different Gospel, p. 172.

[3] Robert L. Thomas, Revelation 1-7 (Moody Press, 2002), p. 51.

[4] Fritz Rienecker and Cleon Rogers, Linguistic Key to the Greek New Testament (Regency, 1980), p. 811.

[5] Donald Grey Barnhouse, Revelation: God's Last Word (Zondervan, 1971), p.15.

[6] Edward Hindson, Revelation: Unlocking the Future (AMG Publishers, 2002), p. 14.

[7] Ibid.

[8] John MacArthur, Because the Time is Near (Moody, 2007), p. 14.

[9] Harold Willmington, Willmington's Guide to the Bible (Tyndale, 1988), p. 538.

[10] W. Graham Scroggie, The Great Unveiling (Zondervan, 1979), p. 43.

[11] Hindson, p. 52.

[12] MacArthur, p. 20.

[13] Stewart Custer, From Patmos to Paradise (BJU Press, 2004), p. 3.

[14] Thomas L. Constable, "Notes on Revelation 2007 Edition", p. 7, http://www.soniclight.com/constable/notes/pdf/revelation.pdf.

[15] Lehman Strauss, Revelation (Loizeaux Brothers, 1964), p. 23.